The SECOND 100 JAPANESE KANJI

The quick and easy way to learn the basic Japanese kanji

Introduction by
Eriko Sato

TUTTLE PUBLISHING
Tokyo • Rutland, Vermont • Singapore

Published by Tuttle Publishing, an imprint of Periplus Editions (HK) Ltd., with editorial offices at 364 Innovation Drive, North Clarendon, Vermont 05759 U.S.A.

ISBN: 978-4-8053-1009-0

Distributed by:

North America, Latin America & Europe
Tuttle Publishing
364 Innovation Drive
North Clarendon, VT 05759-9436 U.S.A.
Tel: 1 (802) 773-8930
Fax: 1 (802) 773-6993
info@tuttlepublishing.com
www.tuttlepublishing.com

Japan
Tuttle Publishing
Yaekari Building, 3rd Floor
5-4-12 Osaki
Shinagawa-ku
Tokyo 141 0032
Tel: (81) 3 5437-0171
Fax: (81) 3 5437-0755
tuttle-sales@gol.com

Asia Pacific
Berkeley Books Pte. Ltd.
61 Tai Seng Avenue #02-12
Singapore 534167
Tel: (65) 6280-1330
Fax: (65) 6280-6290
inquiries@periplus.com.sg
www.periplus.com

First edition
13 12 11 10 09
10 9 8 7 6 5 4 3 2 1

Printed in Singapore

Contents

Introduction

Modern Japanese can be written horizontally, from left to right, or vertically, from top to bottom. Japanese is one of the rare languages that uses multiple writing systems simultaneously, sometimes even in the same sentence. It is written by combining Chinese characters, called *kanji*, and two sets of syllabic alphabets called *kana* (*hiragana* and *katakana*) along with a few punctuation marks. Each kanji character represents a meaning, while each kana character represents a sound. For example, the following short sentence contains kanji, hiragana, and katakana:

パーティーに来ました。
Pātī ni kimashita.
(He) came to the party.

The non-Chinese loanword パーティー, written **pātī** in Roman letters and meaning *party*, is written in katakana. The stem of the verb 来, pronounced *ki* and meaning *to come*, is written using kanji. The grammatical particle に, written **ni** in Roman letters and meaning *to*, and the inflectional element ました, pronounced **mashita** (polite past affirmative), are written in hiragana. Isn't it interesting that all three writing systems can be used in such a simple sentence?

The total number of kana is relatively small: there are only 46 basic characters for each kana system in modern Japanese. By contrast, the total number of kanji is quite large. The Japanese government selected a total of 1,945 kanji (the so-called **jōyō** kanji, or kanji for daily use) in 1981. Japanese students are expected to learn how to read all of these kanji by the time they graduate high school. Additional kanji are used in proper names and certain other words.

You might think that there are too many kanji characters to learn, but don't get discouraged! If you learn the first several hundred kanji characters, you will be able to understand or guess the meaning of most street signs, restaurant menus, merchandise names, a variety of instructions, and much more! Furthermore, it is a lot of fun to learn kanji because the characters have interesting historical and cultural backgrounds and amazing compositional structures. Each kanji character has a unique meaning and shape, so each time you learn a new kanji character, you'll feel a bit like you've made a new friend.

The key to your ultimate success is to learn the basic kanji correctly and solidly. Start with the ones that appear in *The First 100 Japanese Kanji*, the companion volume to this one. You'll find the second 100 kanji can be learned more easily than the first 100, the third 100 kanji can be learned even more easily than the second 100, and so on. You can see how important it is to start with a solid foundation. Welcome to *The Second 100 Japanese Kanji*! If you make a manageable plan for learning with this workbook everyday, you'll be able to enjoy the process of learning

kanji and greatly improve your reading proficiency in Japanese. This introduction provides you with the information you need to know about the development and use of kanji and shows you how to write them properly.

How did kanji develop?
The word **kanji** literally means "characters of the Han Dynasty of ancient China" (206 B.C.E. to 220 A.D.). The initial forms of kanji originated in the Yellow River region of China between 2000 and 1500 B.C.E. The earliest preserved characters were written on tortoise shells and animal bones. About 3,000 characters have been discovered from this early period. Depending on how they were formed, kanji can be classified into four main categories: pictorial kanji, indicative kanji, compound ideographic kanji, and phonetic-ideographic kanji.

Pictorial kanji originated from pictures of objects or phenomena. For example:

Meaning	Original Picture	Modern Kanji
River		川
Mountain		山
Tree		木
Sun		日
Moon		月
Rain		雨

Indicative kanji were created as symbolic representations of abstract concepts using points and lines. For example:

Meaning	Original Sign	Modern Kanji
One		一
Two		二
Three		三
Top		上
Bottom		下

Compound ideographic kanji were formed by combining two or more pictorial or indicative kanji to bring out a new but simple idea. For example:

Meaning	Combining Multiple Kanji	Resulting Kanji
Woods	木 + 木 tree + tree	林
Forest	木 + 木 + 木 tree + tree + tree	森
Bright	日 + 月 sun + moon	明

Finally, *phonetic-ideographic kanji* were formed by combining an element that expressed meaning and an element that carried the sound. For example, the following characters all stand for some body of water:

Meaning	Combining Elements	Kanji
Inlet	氵 + 工 water + KŌ	江
Ocean	氵 + 羊 water + YŌ	洋
River	氵 + 可 water + KA	河

The left side of each character above, 氵, contributes the meaning, showing that each kanji's meaning is related to water. The right side of each character, 工, 羊, or 可, contributes the sound, showing how the kanji should be pronounced.

Kanji characters were brought to Japan from China between the fourth and the fifth centuries A.D. Until then, there were no written symbols in Japanese. The Japanese initially developed a hybrid system where kanji were given Japanese pronunciations and were used for writing Japanese. This system proved unwieldy, since Japanese and Chinese grammar and structure are so different. Then, they developed a system, **man'yōgana**, in which a limited set of kanji was used to write Japanese words with their sounds. Hiragana and katakana were developed in the Heian Period (794-1185) from some of the kanji characters included in **man'yōgana**. About 2,000 kanji as well as hiragana and katakana are still used in modern Japanese. Interestingly, there are some kanji characters that were created in Japan. For example, the kanji 峠 (mountain pass), 畑 (field of crops), and 働 (work) were all created in Japan by combining multiple existing kanji components.

How are kanji pronounced?

The Japanese language is very different from the Chinese language, having very distinct grammar and sounds. Many Chinese words consist of one syllable, but most Japanese words have more than one syllable. So, the assignment of a Japanese pronunciation to each kanji required both flexibility and creativity.

On-readings and kun-readings

There are two different ways of reading kanji in Japanese: on-readings (or **on-yomi**) and kun-readings (or **kun-yomi**). When kanji characters were first introduced to Japan, the original Chinese pronunciations were also adapted with only minor modifications. Such Chinese ways of reading kanji are called on-readings and are still used, especially when a character appears as a part of a compound where two or more kanji are combined to form a word.

At the same time, many kanji characters were assigned the pronunciation of the existing native Japanese word whose meaning was closest to that of the character. Such Japanese readings are called kun-readings, and are used especially when a character occurs independently in a sentence. For example, the character 母 is pronounced **bo** (on-reading) when used as a part of the compound word 母国, **bokoku** (mother country), but is pronounced **haha** (kun-reading) when used by itself. This is illustrated in the following sentence.

私の母の母国はフランスです。
Watashi no haha no bokoku wa Furansu desu.
My mother's mother country is France.

In this workbook, on-readings are shown in katakana and, when Romanized, in upper-case letters. Conversely, kun-readings are shown in hiragana and in lower-case letters when Romanized.

Some kanji characters have more than one on-reading or kun-reading, and different readings are used in different contexts. Also note that there are special cases where it is not possible to clearly divide a kanji compound into components that can be pronounced separately.

Okurigana

As noted above, many Chinese words consist of a single syllable, expressed by only one Chinese character, but the corresponding Japanese words often have more than one syllable. In order to use kanji in the Japanese language, some kanji characters needed to be accompanied by kana. Such kana are called **okurigana**. Okurigana are particularly important for verbs and adjectives, which need inflectional elements, although they may also be used for other types of words, including nouns and adverbs. For example, in the following words, the kanji 高, meaning *expensive* or *high*, and the kana that follow jointly represent the pronunciation of the whole word, successfully representing its complete meaning:

高い	takai	expensive (plain present affirmative)
高くない	takakunai	not expensive (plain present negative)
高かった	takakatta	was expensive (plain past affirmative)

In this book, the okurigana are preceded by "–" when first presented in kun-readings.

Furigana

Kanji characters are occasionally provided with kana that shows how they are intended to be read in the given context. Such kana used as a pronunciation guide are called **furigana**. For example, the hiragana characters placed right above the kanji in the following word are furigana:

たか
高い

Furigana is often used for children or learners of Japanese. This can be a great help for you at the beginning! It is also used in newspapers for unusual readings and for characters not included in the officially recognized set of essential kanji. Japanese comic books use furigana generously!

How are kanji used in compounds?

Some Japanese words are represented by only one kanji (e.g., 赤, **aka**, *red*), but many Japanese words are represented by a kanji with okurigana (e.g., 高い, **takai**, *expensive*) or by a kanji compound. Kanji compounds constitute a large proportion of Japanese vocabulary. For example, 先生, written **sensei** in Roman letters, is a compound meaning *teacher*. It consists of two characters, 先 (ahead) and 生 (live). In general, on-readings are used for compounds, but occasionally, kun-readings are also used.

By the way, when you write a compound, there is no need to add a space between the kanji characters in it, but don't try to squeeze the characters together to fit in one-character space. Each character in a compound should take one-character space. For example, notice the difference between 女子(girl) and 好(to like). The first item (女子) is a kanji compound that consists of two kanji characters, 女 (woman) and 子(child). By contrast, the second item (好) is a single kanji character that consists of two kanji components, 女and 子.

Some kanji compounds were created in Japan and have been brought back to China and are now being used there. Examples include 電話 **denwa** (telephone), 化学 **kagaku** (science), and 社会 **shakai** (society). Many kanji compounds are also used to represent Japanese culture, concepts, and ideas (e.g., 神道 **Shinto**) as well as to name Japanese people (e.g., 田中 **Tanaka**), institutions and companies (e.g., 三菱 **Mitsubishi**), places (e.g., 東京 **Tokyo**), and eras (e.g., 明治 **Meiji**). Regardless of their origin, kanji compounds form an essential part of the lives of Japanese people.

There are two special cases where you may have a hard time reading kanji compounds: **jukujikun** and **ateji**. A **jukujikun** is a unique kun-reading assigned to an entire kanji compound rather than to each kanji character separately. For example, the compound 明日 (tomorrow) can be read as **myōnichi** using the on-reading of each character in the compound one after another, as in the majority of typical kanji compounds, but can also be read as **asu**, which is a **jukujikun**. In the latter case, it is impossible to tell which syllable corresponds to 明 and which syllable corresponds to 日 because the reading is assigned to the whole compound. Other examples of **jukujikun** include 一日 **tsuitachi** (the first day of the month), 五月雨 **samidare** (early summer rain), 海老 **ebi** (shrimp), and 土産 **miyage** (souvenir).

Ateji are kanji characters whose sounds are used to represent native Japanese words or non-Chinese loanwords regardless of the meanings of the kanji. For example, the kanji compound 寿司 is made of **ateji**. It is pronounced **sushi**, and means sushi, the food, even though 寿 means *one's natural life span* and 司 means *to administer*, neither of which are directly related to food. Other examples of **ateji** include 目出度い **medetai** (happy), 出鱈目 **deta-rame** (random), and 珈琲 **kōhī** (coffee). Many **ateji** for non-Chinese loanwords, including proper names, have been replaced by katakana, but some are still used. In addition, new **ateji** are occasionally created.

What are radicals?

Most kanji characters are composed of two or more components. Each component may contribute to the kanji's meaning, sound, or merely its shape. For example, 日 is an independent kanji character meaning *sun*, but is also a component that lends meaning to many kanji. For example:

明 *bright*   時 *time*   晴 *clear up*

There are many kanji-components, but the most basic and identifiable elements of kanji are called *radicals*. For hundreds of years, Chinese dictionaries have organized kanji characters according to their radicals. Each Chinese character was assigned a radical and placed in an appropriate section of a dictionary according to the designated radical.

It is not always clear which component of a kanji is the radical, but this workbook shows the radical for each kanji at the upper right corner of the page. Whenever you learn a new kanji using this book, check its radical. It will help you understand and remember the meaning and the internal composition of the kanji. Eventually, you will be able to identify the radical just by looking at a kanji. There is an index of characters organized by radical near the end of this book.

Depending on its position in a kanji character, radicals are classified into seven categories, as shown in the chart on the opposite page:

Name	Position		Example
偏 **hen** (lit., partial, one-sided)	left		イ にんべん **ninben** (person) 休 (rest), 体(body), 作(make)
旁 **tsukuri** (lit., aside)	right		斤 おのづくり **onozukuri** (ax) 近 (near), 新 (new), 所 (place)
冠 **kanmuri** (lit., crown)	top		艹 くさかんむり **kusakanmuri** (grass) 草 (grass), 花 (flower), 茶 (tea)
脚 **ashi** (lit., leg)	bottom		儿 ひとあし **hitoashi** (human legs) 見 (look), 兄 (older brother), 先 (ahead)
構 **kamae** (lit., enclosure)	frame		囗 くにがまえ **kunigamae** (border) 国 (country), 困 (be in difficulty), 囚 (prisoner)
			門 もんがまえ **mongamae** (gate) 問 (inquire), 聞 (listen), 間 (between)
			凵 うけばこ **ukebako** (container, vessel) 画 (picture), 凶 (bad), 歯 (tooth)
			匚 かくしがまえ **kakushigamae** (conceal) 区 (ward), 医 (physician), 匿 (conceal)
			勹 つつみがまえ **tsutsumigamae** (wrap) 包 (wrap), 抱 (embrace), 句 (phrase)
垂 **tare** (lit., something hanging down)	top & left		疒 やまいだれ **yamaidare** (sickness) 病 (illness), 痛 (painful), 癌 (cancer)
繞 **nyō, nyū** (lit., going around)	left & bottom		辶 しんにょう **shinnyō** (proceed) 道 (road), 進 (proceed), 過 (pass)

How do I look up a kanji in a Japanese dictionary?
Many dictionaries list kanji characters according to their pronunciation, for both on-readings and kun-readings, either in kana or in Roman letters. So, if you know the reading of a kanji character, you can easily find it in such a dictionary using its pronunciation-based index. For example, *The Original Modern Reader's Japanese-English Character Dictionary* by Andrew N. Nelson (Tuttle Publishing), has an on/kun index in the back, and kanji characters are alphabetically listed according to both their on-readings and their kun-readings in Roman letters with a unique code number provided for each character. Using that code number, you can easily find the page you should go to in the dictionary.

What if you see a kanji, but you don't know how to read it? You could then use the radical index included in most dictionaries. In a radical index, hundreds of radicals are listed according to the radical's total number of strokes. For example, 日 is the radical of 明, and it has 4 strokes. You can find the radical 日 in the radical list under the section for four-stroke radicals in just a few seconds. There you will find a code number, which will guide you to the list of all the kanji with the radical 日. For example, you will see many kanji, including 明, 晴, and 時, on the page specified by the code number for the radical 日. They are ordered according to their total stroke count. You can easily find the kanji character you want in the list.

If you have no clue about either the pronunciation or the

radical of the kanji, you can use the kanji's total stroke count as a reference. This book specifies the total stroke count for each kanji at the right upper corner of each page, but if you always write kanji in the correct stroke order and with the correct stroke count, you can figure it out by yourself.

How are kanji characters written?
To write kanji properly and legibly, it is very important to know how each stroke in a kanji is drawn. Here are some principles and tendencies for stroke endings, stroke directions, and stroke orders.

Stroke Endings
Each stroke ends in とめ **tome** (stop), はね **hane** (jump), or はらい **harai** (sweep). (Note that some diagonal lines end in stop-sweep.) For example, a vertical straight line can end in stop, jump, or sweep, as shown below:

とめ **tome** (stop)	はね **hane** (jump)	はらい **harai** (sweep)

Stroke Directions
A stroke can be vertical, horizontal, diagonal, angled, or curved, or can be just a short abbreviated line.

Vertical lines always go from top to bottom, and *horizontal lines* always go from left to right.

Diagonal lines can go either downward or upward. For example:

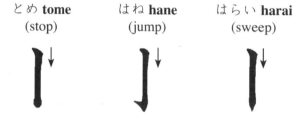

If a stroke forms a corner, a sharp angle, or a curve, it goes from left to right and then goes down, or goes down and then left to right. For example:

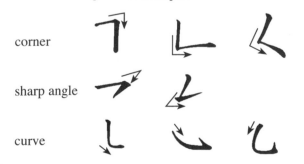

corner

sharp angle

curve

Some strokes have a combination of a sharp angle and a curve. For example:

Some strokes are extremely short and are called てん **ten**. They may be vertical or slightly diagonal:

Stroke Order
You should remember how the strokes in each character are ordered in order to write a character neatly with the appropriate shape. Most kanji characters are written following the general principles of stroke order:

1. Kanji are written from top to bottom.

   三 (three)

2. Kanji are written from left to right.

   川 (river)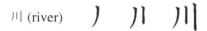

3. Horizontal strokes usually precede vertical strokes when crossing, although there are some exceptions such as 王 and 田.

   十 (ten)

4. A central line usually precedes the strokes placed on its right and left.

   小 (small)

5. An outer frame must be written first before finishing the inside except for the bottom line. The bottom line of an outer frame must be completed at the very end.

   国 (country)

6. A right-to-left diagonal stroke precedes a left-to-right diagonal stroke.

   人 (person)

7. A vertical line piercing through the center of a character is written last.

車 (vehicle)

8. A horizontal line piercing the center of the character is written last.

子 (child)

How do I learn to write kanji?

Remember that a good beginning and good planning are the keys to success in learning kanji. The following are some suggested steps for learning kanji using this workbook.

Get used to the strokes

Before writing any kanji, practice drawing some of the simple strokes with different endings many times on a sheet of scrap paper. For example, try drawing the strokes presented above (e.g., vertical lines, diagonal lines). Each time you end the stroke, say とめ **tome** (stop), はね **hane** (jump), or はらい **harai** (sweep), depending on which type of ending you are working on. If you have a brush and ink, try to make changes in the thickness of different portions of each stroke. Of course, you can also use a pen or pencil. If you do, ignore the difference in the thickness of different portions of each stroke. Just get used to the general flow of strokes. It will help you to write kanji beautifully in an authentic style.

Understand the character

Before writing an actual kanji character as a whole, familiarize yourself with its meaning, pronunciation, usage examples, and radical. Be creative and make associations to help you remember the shape, composition, meaning, and sound of the character you are working on. Your associations can be logical or natural, or can be silly or funny. Your imagination and creativity will always help you learn and remember new things, especially when you are dealing with numerous items. Under each character in this book, the first several boxes show the stroke order and direction. Refer to them, and try writing the character once. The number of strokes for each kanji is specified in the upper-right corner of each page. Check whether you used the correct number of strokes when you wrote the kanji. Then compare your character with the one printed on the page. Pay attention to the size and the position of the character in relation with the box as well as the proportion and shape of the lines.

Practice writing the character

When you have fully understood the given character in terms of meaning, pronunciation, usage, radical, and stroke order, write it about 10 times in a row. You may not believe it, but your hand muscle will remember how to write a kanji if you repeat writing it many times. If helpful, trace over the gray characters at the beginning of each page.

Review kanji periodically

Practice a few new characters at a time every day following the above steps. At the end of each week, review all of the characters you learned during the week by writing them five times each. At the end of each month, review all the characters you learned during the month by writing them a few times each. If you study kanji at this pace using this workbook, you can master 100 new kanji within a month or two! Sounds like a manageable plan, right? Make sure to periodically review the kanji you have learned. Flash cards can be useful, but you can also write the kanji you learned previously again and again to review them. That's why there are plenty of boxes on each page of this workbook! The point is to make an effort daily with a manageable plan for learning and reviewing kanji. Believe it or not, the more you learn, the easier it gets!

頑張ってください。
Ganbatte kudasai!
Try your best (and good luck)!

	ON readings ケン **KEN** KUN readings いぬ **inu**	meaning dog	4 strokes
			radical 犬

犬

common words

愛犬	あいけん	**aiken**	one's pet dog
こま犬	こまいぬ	**komainu**	a pair of stone guardian dogs 　(at the gate of a Shinto shrine)
子犬	こいぬ	**koinu**	puppy
野良犬	のらいぬ	**norainu**	a stray dog; an ownerless dog
負け犬	まけいぬ	**makeinu**	loser
番犬	ばんけん	**banken**	watchdog
もうどう犬	もうどうけん	**mōdōken**	a guide dog (for the blind)

一　ナ　大　犬　犬　犬　犬

	ON readings ギュウ **GYŪ** KUN readings うし **ushi**	meanings cow; bull	4 strokes
			radical 牛

牛

common words

雄牛	おうし	**o'ushi**	ox; bull
牛革	ぎゅうがわ	**gyūgawa**	cowskin; calfskin
牛丼	ぎゅうどん	**gyūdon**	a bowl of rice topped with cooked beef
牛肉	ぎゅうにく	**gyūniku**	beef
牛乳	ぎゅうにゅう	**gyūnyū**	milk
闘牛	とうぎゅう	**tōgyū**	bullfighting
水牛	すいぎゅう	**suigyū**	water buffalo

ノ　ⸯ　⸗　牛　牛　牛　牛

ON readings ギョ **GYO** KUN readings うお **uo,** さかな **sakana**	meaning fish	11 strokes
		radical 魚

魚

common words

魚河岸	うおがし	**uogashi**	fish market
魚の目	うおのめ	**uonome**	corn (growth on a foot)
川魚	かわうお/ かわざかな	**kawa'uo/** **kawazakana**	river [freshwater] fish
魚介	ぎょかい	**gyokai**	seafood
金魚	きんぎょ	**kingyo**	goldfish
雑魚	ざこ	**zako**	small fish; small fry
人魚	にんぎょ	**ningyo**	mermaid; merman

		ON readings チョウ **CHŌ** KUN readings とり **tori**	meaning bird	**11 strokes**
				radical 鳥

鳥

common words

一石二鳥	いっせきにちょう	**isseki nichō**	killing two birds with one stone
小鳥	ことり	**kotori**	small bird
七面鳥	しちめんちょう	**shichimenchō**	turkey
鳥居	とりい	**tori'i**	*torii*; gateway to a Shinto shrine
鳥かご	とりかご	**torikago**	birdcage
焼き鳥	やきとり	**yakitori**	barbecued chicken (on a skewer)
渡り鳥	わたりどり	**wataridori**	migratory bird

人	ON readings ジン **JIN,** ニン **NIN** KUN readings ひと **hito**	meaning person	2 strokes
			radical
			人（イ）

common words

アメリカ人	アメリカじん	**Amerikajin**	American (person)
悪人	あくにん	**akunin**	bad [wicked] person; villain
偉人	いじん	**ijin**	great person; hero
一人前	いちにんまえ	**ichininmae**	one serving
恋人	こいびと	**koibito**	sweetheart; boy/girlfriend
個人	こじん	**kojin**	individual
人形	にんぎょう	**ningyō**	doll; puppet

ノ 人 人 人 人

	ON readings ドウ **DŌ** KUN readings うご-かす **ugo-kasu,** うご-く **ugo-ku**	meaning to move	**11 strokes** radical 力

common words

自動車	じどうしゃ	**jidōsha**	automobile; car
移動	いどう	**idō**	movement
運動	うんどう	**undō**	movement; exercise; sports
活動	かつどう	**katsudō**	activity
感動する	かんどうする	**kandō suru**	be impressed with
行動する	こうどうする	**kōdō suru**	to act
動物	どうぶつ	**dōbutsu**	animal
動詞	どうし	**dōshi**	verb

一₁	三₂	三₃	戸₄	戸₅	重₆	重₇	重₈
重₉	動₁₀	動₁₁	動	動	動		

	ON readings ニク **NIKU** KUN readings	meanings fresh; meat	**6 strokes** radical 肉

common words

筋肉	きんにく	**kin'niku**	muscle
鳥肉	とりにく	**toriniku**	chicken
肉体	にくたい	**nikutai**	the body; the flesh
肉屋	にくや	**nikuya**	butcher; meat shop
ひき肉	ひきにく	**hikiniku**	ground [minced] meat
焼き肉	やきにく	**yakiniku**	grilled meat
皮肉	ひにく	**hiniku**	irony

肉

	ON readings シ SHI KUN readings かみ kami	meaning paper	**10 strokes**
			radical 糸

紙

common words

手紙	てがみ	**tegami**	letter
折り紙	おりがみ	**origami**	origami; folding paper
型紙	かたがみ	**katagami**	paper [dress] pattern
色紙	いろがみ/しきし	**irogami/shikishi**	colored paper/square piece of Japanese paper
紙幣	しへい	**shihei**	paper money; bill
表紙	ひょうし	**hyōshi**	cover
和紙	わし	**washi**	(handmade) Japanese paper
紙くず	かみくず	**kamikuzu**	wastepaper

	ON readings	meanings	5 strokes
	ホン **HON**	book; main;	
	KUN readings	true; counter for	**radical**
	もと **moto**	long objects	木

本

common words

日本人	にほんじん	**Nihonjin**	Japanese person
絵本	えほん	**ehon**	picture book
基本	きほん	**kihon**	basis; foundation
製本	せいほん	**seihon**	bookbinding
本店	ほんてん	**honten**	head [main] office
本当に	ほんとうに	**hontō ni**	really; truly; actually
本物	ほんもの	**hon'mono**	real thing
本屋	ほんや	**hon'ya**	bookstore

一 十 才 木 本 本 本 本

	ON readings セイ SEI, ショウ SHŌ KUN readings いーきる i-kiru, いーかす i-kasu, いーける i-keru, うーまれる u-mareru, うーむ u-mu, おーう o-u, はーえる ha-eru, はーやす ha-yasu, き ki, なま nama	meanings birth; life	5 strokes
生			radical 生

common words

生物	せいぶつ	**seibutsu**	living thing; creature; life
一生	いっしょう	**isshō**	lifetime; one's whole life
生まれる	うまれる	**umareru**	be born; to arise; to appear
生地	きじ	**kiji**	cloth; fabric; textile
写生	しゃせい	**shasei**	sketching
生活	せいかつ	**seikatsu**	life; living
生える	はえる	**haeru**	to come up; to grow
生ビール	なまビール	**nama biiru**	draft beer

ノ　ー　牛　生　生　生　生　生

	ON readings セン **SEN** KUN readings さき **saki**		meanings future; ahead; point; tip	6 strokes
				radical 儿

先

common words

先生	せんせい	**sensei**	teacher; instructor; master
あて先	あてさき	**atesaki**	address; addressee
先払い	さきばらい	**sakibarai**	advance payment
先日	せんじつ	**senjitsu**	the other day; some days [time] ago
つま先	つまさき	**tsumasaki**	tip of the toe
指先	ゆびさき	**yubisaki**	fingertip
ゆう先	ゆうせん	**yūsen**	priority; precedence

丿 ⟍ ⺧ 牛 先 先 先 先

先

	ON readings ガク **GAKU** KUN readings まな-ぶ **mana-bu**	meanings learning, studies	8 strokes
			radical 子

学

common words

医学	いがく	**igaku**	medicine; medical science
化学	かがく	**kagaku**	chemistry
文学	ぶんがく	**bungaku**	literature
大学	だいがく	**daigaku**	university; college
学習する	がくしゅうする	**gakushū suru**	to learn; to study
学生	がくせい	**gakusei**	student
学者	がくしゃ	**gakusha**	scholar

| ON readings
コウ **KŌ**
KUN readings | meaning
school | **10 strokes** |
| | | radical
木 |

校

common words

学校	がっこう	**gakkō**	school
小学校	しょうがっこう	**shōgakkō**	elementary [primary] school
校長	こうちょう	**kōchō**	school principal
高校	こうこう	**kōkō**	high school
校舎	こうしゃ	**kōsha**	school building
校正	こうせい	**kōsei**	proofreading
校庭	こうてい	**kōtei**	school grounds
母校	ぼこう	**bokō**	alma mater

一 十 才 木 木 朼 朼 杧

杧 校 校 校 校

	ON readings カ KA KUN readings	meanings academic course; department; section	9 strokes
			radical 禾

科

common words

科学	かがく	**kagaku**	science
学科	がっか	**gakka**	subject; course
教科	きょうか	**kyōka**	subject; course of study; curriculum
眼科	がんか	**ganka**	ophthalmology
百科事典	ひゃっかじてん	**hyakkajiten**	encyclopedia
歯科	しか	**shika**	dental clinic
前科	ぜんか	**zenka**	criminal record

丿 二 千 禾 禾 禾 禾 禾

科 科 科 科

	ON readings リ RI KUN readings	meanings reason; logic	11 strokes
			radical 玉（王）

理

common words

理科	りか	**rika**	natural science
管理	かんり	**kanri**	management; administration
経理	けいり	**keiri**	accounting
修理	しゅうり	**shūri**	repair
代理	だいり	**dairi**	representation
無理な	むりな	**muri na**	unreasonable; impossible
料理	りょうり	**ryōri**	cooking

二　丁　王　王　玘　玕　珥

珥　理　理　理　理　理

	ON readings ゴ **GO** KUN readings かた-らう **kata-rau,** かた-る **kata-ru**	meaning word; language	**14 strokes**
語			radical 言

common words

語る	かたる	**kataru**	to tell; to talk
敬語	けいご	**keigo**	respect speech [language]
語学	ごがく	**gogaku**	language study
言語	げんご	**gengo**	language; speech
国語	こくご	**kokugo**	Japanese language; national language
単語	たんご	**tango**	word; vocabulary
物語	ものがたり	**monogatari**	story; talk

	ON readings エイ **EI** KUN readings	meanings England; English	**8 strokes** radical 艹

英

common words

英語	えいご	**eigo**	English
英会話	えいかいわ	**eikaiwa**	English conversation
英国	えいこく	**Eikoku**	England; the United Kingdom
英文	えいぶん	**eibun**	English language text
英訳	えいやく	**eiyaku**	translation into English
英和辞典	えいわじてん	**eiwajiten**	English-Japanese dictionary
英雄	えいゆう	**eiyū**	hero

一 艹 艹 艹 芇 苩 英 英

英 英 英

| | ON readings
ジ **JI**
KUN readings
あざ **aza** | meaning
letter | **6 strokes**
radical
子 |

字

common words

英字新聞	えいじしんぶん	**eijishinbun**	English newspaper
大文字	おおもじ	**ōmoji**	capital letter
小文字	こもじ	**komoji**	small letter
漢字	かんじ	**kanji**	kanji; Chinese character
活字	かつじ	**katsuji**	type [printing]
習字	しゅうじ	**shūji**	penmanship; calligraphy
文字	もじ	**moji**	character; letter

	ON readings ベン **BEN** KUN readings	meaning effort; to work hard	**10 strokes**
			radical 力

勉

common words

勉強する	べんきょうする	**benkyō suru**	to study
勉強家	べんきょうか	**benkyōka**	hard [good] worker
勤勉	きんべん	**kinben**	diligence
勉学	べんがく	**bengaku**	study
不勉強な	ふべんきょうな	**fubenkyō na**	idle; lazy

	ON readings キョウ **KYŌ**, ゴウ **GŌ** KUN readings つよ－い **tsuyo-i**, つよ－まる **tsuyo-maru**, つよ－める **tsuyo-meru**, し－いる **shi-iru**	meaning strong	**11 strokes** radical 弓

強

common words

強運	きょううん	**kyōun**	good luck
強化する	きょうかする	**kyōka suru**	to strengthen
強引に	ごういんに	**gōin ni**	by force, forcibly
強いる	しいる	**shiiru**	to force; to impose
強がり	つよがり	**tsuyogari**	bluff; bluster
手強い	てごわい	**tegowai**	tough
補強する	ほきょうする	**hokyō suru**	to reinforce

	ON readings こう **KŌ** KUN readings この-む **kono-mu,** す-く **su-ku**	meanings good; fine; favorable	6 strokes
			radical 女

好

common words

格好いい	かっこういい	**kakkō ii**	cool; smart; attractive
好奇心	こうきしん	**kōkishin**	curiosity
好都合な	こうつごうな	**kōtsugō na**	convenient
好物	こうぶつ	**kōbutsu**	favorite food
好み	このみ	**konomi**	liking; taste; choice; preference
好き嫌い	すききらい	**sukikirai**	likes and dislikes
友好	ゆうこう	**yūkō**	friendship; amity

	ON readings シュウ **SHŪ** KUN readings なら－う **nara-u**	meanings to learn; to study	11 strokes
			radical 羽

習

common words

学習	がくしゅう	**gakushū**	learning; study
見習う	みならう	**minarau**	to emulate
自習する	じしゅうする	**jishū suru**	to study by oneself
習慣	しゅうかん	**shūkan**	habit
実習	じっしゅう	**jisshū**	practice
風習	ふうしゅう	**fūshū**	manners; customs
復習	ふくしゅう	**fukushū**	review

	ON readings	meaning	11 strokes
	モン MON	question; inquiry	
	KUN readings		radical
	と−い to-i, と−う to-u, とん ton		口

問

common words

学問	がくもん	**gakumon**	studies
疑問	ぎもん	**gimon**	doubt; question
質問	しつもん	**shitsumon**	question
問い合わせ	といあわせ	**toi'awase**	inquiry
問屋	とんや	**ton'ya**	wholesale store; wholesaler
訪問	ほうもん	**hōmon**	visit
問題	もんだい	**mondai**	question; problem

ON readings トウ **TŌ** **KUN readings** こた-え **kota-e,** こた-える **kota-eru**		**meaning** answer	**12 strokes**
			radical 竹

答

common words

応答	おうとう	**outō**	response; reply; answer
問答	もんどう	**mondō**	questions and answers
解答	かいとう	**kaitō**	answer; solution
答案	とうあん	**tōan**	answer; examination paper
返答	へんとう	**hentō**	answer; reply

	ON readings ガク **GAKU,** ラク **RAKU** KUN readings たのし−い **tanoshi-i,** たのし−む **tanoshi-mu**	meaning music; comfort; ease	13 strokes
			radical 木

楽

common words

安楽	あんらく	**anraku**	comfort; ease
音楽	おんがく	**ongaku**	music
楽団	がくだん	**gakudan**	band; orchestra
楽譜	がくふ	**gakufu**	score
楽屋	がくや	**gakuya**	dressing room
気楽な	きらくな	**kiraku na**	carefree; comfortable
娯楽	ごらく	**goraku**	amusement; recreation
道楽	どうらく	**dōraku**	hobby; dissipation

	ON readings シン SHIN KUN readings あたら-しい atara-shii, あら-た ara-ta, にい nii		meanings new; fresh; latest	13 strokes
				radical 斤

新

common words

新しい	あたらしい	**atarashii**	new; fresh; latest
最新の	さいしんの	**saishin no**	the latest; the newest
新人	しんじん	**shinjin**	newcomer; new face; rookie
新型	しんがた	**shingata**	new style [type]
新記録	しんきろく	**shinkiroku**	new record [document]
新品	しんぴん	**shinpin**	new [brand-new] article
新聞	しんぶん	**shinbun**	newspaper

	ON readings コ **KO** KUN readings ふる−い **furu-i,** ふる−す **furu-su**		meanings old; ancient	**5 strokes**
				radical 口

古

common words

中古の	ちゅうこの	**chūko no**	secondhand; used
お古	おふる	**ofuru**	hand-me-downs
古代	こだい	**kodai**	ancient times; antiquity
古典	こてん	**koten**	classic
最古の	さいこの	**saiko no**	the oldest
古くさい	ふるくさい	**furukusai**	old-fashioned; stale
古ぼけた	ふるぼけた	**furuboketa**	grow old
古本	ふるほん	**furuhon**	second-hand [used] book

一　十　古　古　古　古　古　古

	ON readings エン **EN,** オン **ON** KUN readings とおーい **tō-i**	meanings far; distant	13 strokes
			radical 辶

遠

common words

永遠	えいえん	**ei'en**	eternity; permanence
遠足	えんそく	**ensoku**	excursion; outing; picnic
遠りょする	えんりょする	**enryo suru**	refrain; hesitate
遠く	とおく	**tōku**	far
待ち遠しい	まちどおしい	**machidōshii**	be looking forward to
遠ざかる	とおざかる	**tōzakaru**	to leave
望遠鏡	ぼうえんきょう	**bōenkyō**	telescope

一	十	土	圭	吉	吉	声	袁
1	2	3	4	5	6	7	8

袁	袁	袁	遠	遠	遠	遠	遠
9	10	11	12	13			

| | ON readings
キン **KIN**
KUN readings
ちか−い **chika-i** | meanings
near; close | 7 strokes |
| | | | radical
辶 |

近

common words

近眼	きんがん	**kingan**	nearsightedness
近所	きんじょ	**kinjo**	neighborhood
近代	きんだい	**kindai**	modern times [era]
最近	さいきん	**saikin**	recently
近付く	ちかづく	**chikazuku**	to approach; to close
近い	ちかい	**chikai**	near; close
身近に	みぢかに	**mijika ni**	close (to)

´¹	⌐² 厂	斤³	斤⁴	`斤⁵	斤⁶ 近	近⁷	近
近	近						

	ON readings チョウ CHŌ KUN readings ながーい naga-i	meanings long; a chief	8 strokes
			radical 長

長

common words

延長する	えんちょうする	**enchō suru**	to extend
会長	かいちょう	**kaichō**	chairperson
課長	かちょう	**kachō**	section manager
院長	いんちょう	**inchō**	director (of a hospital)
市長	しちょう	**shichō**	mayor
身長	しんちょう	**shinchō**	height
成長	せいちょう	**seichō**	growth

l	厂	F	E	上	镸	長	長

長	長	長					

短

ON readings
タン **TAN**
KUN readings
みじか-い **mijika-i**

meanings
shortness; defect

12 strokes

radical
矢

common words

最短の	さいたんの	**saitan no**	the shortest
短気な	たんきな	**tanki na**	short temper
短期大学	たんきだいがく	**tanki daigaku**	junior college
短距離	たんきょり	**tankyori**	short distance [range]
短縮	たんしゅく	**tanshuku**	shortening; reduction
短所	たんしょ	**tansho**	fault; weak point
手短な	てみじかな	**temijika na**	short; brief

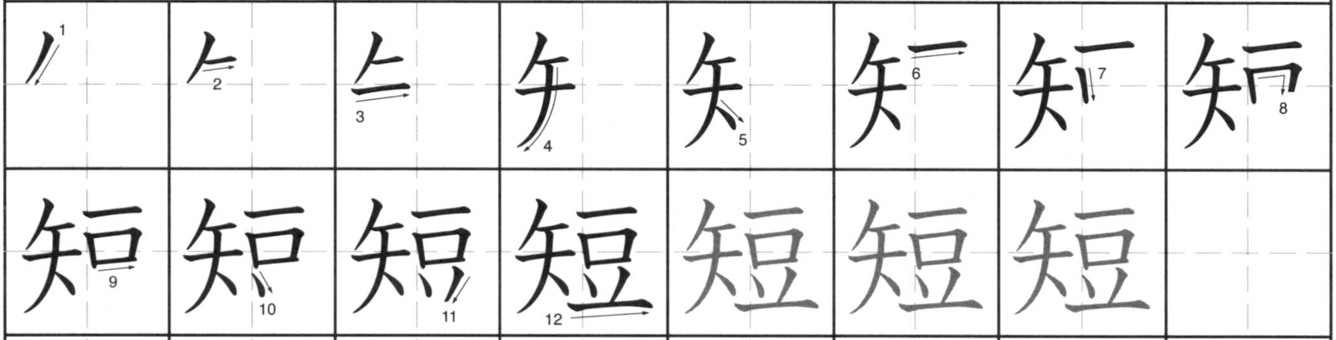

ON readings ソク SOKU KUN readings はや-い haya-i, はや-める haya-meru, すみ-やか sumi-yaka	meanings quick; fast; prompt	10 strokes
		radical ⻌

速

common words

急速な	きゅうそくな	**kyūsoku na**	rapid
高速	こうそく	**kōsoku**	high [full] speed
早速	さっそく	**sassoku**	at once; immediately
速達	そくたつ	**sokutatsu**	special [express] delivery
速度	そくど	**sokudo**	speed
速記	そっき	**sokki**	shorthand
速める	はやめる	**hayameru**	to quicken

一 丆 亓 亘 束 束 束 束

速 速 速 速 速

41

		ON readings	meanings	12 strokes
		チ CHI	late; slow	
		KUN readings		radical
		おそーい oso-i, おくーらす oku-rasu, おくーれる oku-reru		辶

遅

common words

遅れる	おくれる	**okureru**	to be late; to be delayed
遅刻する	ちこくする	**chikoku suru**	to be late
手遅れ	ておくれ	**teokure**	be too late
遅い	おそい	**osoi**	slow
遅延	ちえん	**chien**	delay

⼧ ¹	⼬ ²	⼫ ³	⼫ ⁴	⼫ ⁵	⼫ ⁶	⼫ ⁷	层 ⁸
犀 ⁹	犀 ¹⁰	遅 ¹¹	遅 ¹²	遅	遅	遅	

		ON readings ダイ DAI, タイ TAI KUN readings おお- ō-, おお-きい ō-kii, おお-いに ō-ini	meanings big; large; great	3 strokes
				radical 大

大

common words

大急ぎで	おおいそぎで	**ōisogi de**	in a hurry; rushed
大いに	おおいに	**ōi ni**	very (much); greatly
大掛かりな	おおがかりな	**ōgakari na**	large-scale
大ざっぱな(に)	おおざっぱな(に)	**ōzappa na (ni)**	rough(ly)
大勢	おおぜい	**ōzei**	crowd of people
最大の	さいだいの	**saidai no**	the biggest; the largest
大人	おとな	**otona**	grown-up; adult

一 ナ 大 大 大 大

	ON readings ショウ **SHŌ** KUN readings ちい－さい **chii-sai,** お－ **o-,** こ－ **ko-**	meanings small; little	3 strokes
			radical 小

小

common words

小型の	こがたの	**kogata no**	small; small-sized
小切手	こぎって	**kogitte**	check (bank)
小づかい	こづかい	**kozukai**	pocket money
小包	こづつみ	**kozutsumi**	package
小麦	こむぎ	**komugi**	wheat
小指	こゆび	**koyubi**	pinkie (finger)
小説	しょうせつ	**shōsetsu**	novel; fiction

亅 小 小 小 小 小

	ON readings		meanings	6 strokes
	タ **TA**		many; a lot;	
	KUN readings		plenty of	**radical**
	おおーい **o'o-i**			タ

多

common words

多少	たしょう	**tashō**	number; quantity; some
多数の	たすうの	**tasū no**	a large number of; a lot of
最多	さいた	**saita**	the most
大多数	だいたすう	**daitasū**	large majority
多彩な	たさいな	**tasai na**	colorful

ON readings ショウ **SHŌ** **KUN readings** すく－ない **suku-nai,** すこ－し **suko-shi**		**meanings** few; little	**4 strokes** **radical** 小

少

common words

減少する	げんしょうする	**genshō suru**	to decrease
最年少	さいねんしょう	**sainenshō**	the youngest
少年	しょうねん	**shōnen**	boy
少数	しょうすう	**shōsū**	small number
少量	しょうりょう	**shōryō**	small quantity (of)
少ない	すくない	**sukunai**	a few; a little
少々	しょうしょう	**shōshō**	a little; a few

丿 小 小 少 少 少 少

	ON readings		meanings	4 strokes
	タ **TA**, タイ **TAI**		fat; thick; deep (voice); bold (lines)	radical
	KUN readings			
	ふと-い **futo-i**, ふと-る **futo-ru**			大

太

common words

図太い	ずぶとい	**zubutoi**	bold; impudent
太陽	たいよう	**taiyō**	the sun
太字	ふとじ	**futoji**	boldface (type)
丸太	まるた	**maruta**	log
太平洋	たいへいよう	**Taiheiyō**	the Pacific Ocean
太もも	ふともも	**futomomo**	thigh
太った	ふとった	**futotta**	fat

一 ナ 大 太 太 太 太

		ON readings セイ **SEI**, ショウ **SHŌ** KUN readings まさ-に **masa-ni,** ただ-しい **tada-shii,** ただ-す **tada-su**	meanings right; correct; proper	5 strokes
				radical 止

正

common words

修正する	しゅうせいする	**shūsei suru**	to amend; to revise
正月	しょうがつ	**Shōgatsu**	January 1st; the New Year
正直な	しょうじきな	**shōjiki na**	honest
正面	しょうめん	**shōmen**	the front
正確な(に)	せいかくな(に)	**seikaku na (ni)**	correct(ly); exact(ly)
正義	せいぎ	**seigi**	justice
正しい	ただしい	**tadashii**	right; correct; proper; honest

一　丁　下　正　正　正　正　正

	ON readings コウ **KŌ** KUN readings ひろ－い **hiro-i,** ひろ－まる **hiro-maru,** ひろ－める **hiro-meru,** ひろ－がる **hiro-garu,** ひろ－げる **hiro-geru**	meanings wide; large; broad	5 strokes
			radical 广

広

common words

広告	こうこく	**kōkoku**	advertisement; notice
広大な	こうだいな	**kōdai na**	vast
幅広い	はばひろい	**habahiroi**	wide; broad
広がる	ひろがる	**hirogaru**	to spread (out); to widen
広げる	ひろげる	**hirogeru**	to spread; to open
広場	ひろば	**hiroba**	open space
背広	せびろ	**sebiro**	business suit

丶	亠	广	広	広	広	広	広

	ON readings	meanings	6 strokes
	アン AN	cheap; inexpensive; secure; to feel relieved	
安	KUN readings やすーい yasu-i		radical 宀

common words

安易な	あんいな	**an'i na**	easy; easygoing
安定した	あんていした	**anteishita**	stable; steady
安静	あんせい	**ansei**	rest; quiet
安全	あんぜん	**anzen**	safety; security
気安い	きやすい	**kiyasui**	friendly; familiar
不安	ふあん	**fuan**	anxiety; worry
安売り	やすうり	**yasu'uri**	(bargain) sale

	ON readings コウ **KŌ** KUN readings たかーい **taka-i,** たか **taka,** たかーまる **taka-maru,** たかーめる **taka-meru**		meanings high; expensive	**10 strokes**
高				radical 高

common words

高温	こうおん	**kō'on**	high temperature
高価な	こうかな	**kōka na**	expensive
高級な	こうきゅうな	**kōkyū na**	high-quality; luxury
高山	こうざん	**kōzan**	high mountain
最高の	さいこうの	**saikō no**	highest; maximum
残高	ざんだか	**zandaka**	balance
高さ	たかさ	**takasa**	height

＇ 1	亠 2	宀 3	古 4	古 5	古 6	高 7
高 8	高 9	高 10	高	高		

	ON readings ソウ **SŌ** KUN readings はや-い **haya-i,** はや-まる **haya-maru,** はや-める **haya-meru**	meanings early; soon; fast; rapid; quick	6 strokes radical 日

早

common words

お早う	おはよう	**Ohayō.**	Good morning.
早送り	はやおくり	**hayaokuri**	fast-forward
素早い	すばやい	**subayai**	quick
早急な(に)	そうきゅうな(に)	**sōkyū na (ni)**	immediate(ly); prompt(ly)
早朝	そうちょう	**sōchō**	early morning
早起き	はやおき	**hayaoki**	early riser
早業	はやわざ	**hayawaza**	quick work

丨	冂	日	旦	旦	早	早	早
1	2	3	4	5	6		

早							

	ON readings メイ **MEI,** ミョウ **MYŌ** KUN readings あか-り **aka-ri,** あか-るい **aka-rui,** あき-らか **aki-raka,** あ-ける **a-keru,** あ-く **a-ku,** あ-くる **a-kuru,** あ-かす **a-kasu**	meaning bright	8 strokes radical 日

明

common words

明かり	あかり	**akari**	light
明らかな	あきらかな	**akiraka na**	clear; obvious
明ける	あける	**akeru**	to break; to be over; to dawn, to break (day)
発明	はつめい	**hatsumei**	invention
打ち明ける	うちあける	**uchi'akeru**	to confide
照明	しょうめい	**shōmei**	lighting
説明する	せつめいする	**setsumei suru**	to explain

丨	冂	日	日	明	明	明	明
明	明	明					

入	**ON readings** ニュウ **NYŪ** **KUN readings** いーる **i-ru,** いーれる **i-reru,** はいーる **hai-ru**	**meanings** entering; attendance	**2 strokes** radical 入

common words

入り口	いりぐち	**iriguchi**	entrance; door
記入する	きにゅうする	**kinyū suru**	to enter; to fill out
入学する	にゅうがくする	**nyūgaku suru**	to enter a school; to enroll
仕入れ	しいれ	**shi'ire**	purchasing
収入	しゅうにゅう	**shūnyū**	income; earnings
入会	にゅうかい	**nyūkai**	admission
入国	にゅうこく	**nyūkoku**	entry [entrance] (into a country)

	ON readings シュツ SHUTSU, スイ SUI KUN readings でーる de-ru, だーす da-su	meaning to come out; to go out	5 strokes
出	**common words** 出口　　　でぐち　　　　**deguchi**　　　exit 家出する　いえでする　　**iede suru**　　to run away 売り出し　うりだし　　　**uridashi**　　special sale 思い出　　おもいで　　　**omoide**　　　memory 貸し出し　かしだし　　　**kashidashi**　loan; lending 出産　　　しゅっさん　　**shussan**　　(child) birth 出席する　しゅっせきする　**shusseki suru**　to attend 出発　　　しゅっぱつ　　**shuppatsu**　departure		

丨	屮	屮	出	出	出	出	出

	ON readings イン **IN** KUN readings ひーく **hi-ku,** ひーける **hi-keru**	meaning pull	4 strokes
			radical 弓

引

common words

引退	いんたい	**intai**	retirement
引用	いんよう	**in'yō**	quotation
強引な	ごういんな	**gōin na**	forcible
さく引	さくいん	**sakuin**	index
取り引き	とりひき	**torihiki**	business; trade
引っかく	ひっかく	**hikkaku**	to scratch
割引	わりびき	**waribiki**	discount

	ON readings シ **SHI** KUN readings と−まる **to-maru,** と−める **to-meru,** や−む **ya-mu,** や−める **ya-meru**	meaning to stop	4 strokes
止			radical 止

common words

受け止める	うけとめる	**uketomeru**	to catch; to receive
禁止する	きんしする	**kinshi suru**	to forbid; to prohibit
中止する	ちゅうしする	**chūshi suru**	to stop
防止	ぼうし	**bōshi**	prevention
止む	やむ	**yamu**	to stop; to die down; to die away
止める	やめる	**yameru**	to stop; to quit; to cancel
引き止める	ひきとめる	**hikitomeru**	to keep

丨	卜	止	止	止	止	止	

	ON readings ソウ **SŌ** KUN readings はし−る **hashi-ru**	meaning to run	7 strokes
			radical 走

走

common words

競走	きょうそう	**kyōsō**	race
脱走	だっそう	**dassō**	escape
走者	そうしゃ	**sōsha**	runner
逃走する	とうそうする	**tōsō suru**	to escape; to run away
口走る	くちばしる	**kuchibashiru**	to blurt out; to babble

1	十 2	土 3	キ 4	キ 5	走 6	走 7	走
走	走						

	ON readings ホ **HO,** ブ **BU** **KUN readings** ある−く **aru-ku,** あゆ−む **ayu-mu**	**meanings** to walk; to step	**8 strokes** radical 止

歩

common words

歩み	あゆみ	**ayumi**	walking; pace; course
歩く	あるく	**aruku**	to walk; to step
散歩	さんぽ	**sanpo**	walk; stroll
初歩	しょほ	**shoho**	the rudiments; the elements
進歩	しんぽ	**shinpo**	progress (in); advancement; improvement
出歩く	であるく	**dearuku**	to go out
歩道	ほどう	**hodō**	sidewalk

| | ON readings
セツ SETSU, サイ SAI
KUN readings
き－る ki-ru, き－れる ki-reru | meaning
to cut | 4 strokes |
| | | | radical
刀 |

切

common words

一切	いっさい	**issai**	all; everything; nothing
裏切り者	うらぎりもの	**uragirimono**	traitor; betrayer
売り切れる	うりきれる	**urikireru**	to be sold out; to be out of stock
切り取る	きりとる	**kiritoru**	to cut off; to tear off
切手	きって	**kitte**	(postage) stamp
切符	きっぷ	**kippu**	ticket
大切な	たいせつな	**taisetsu na**	important; precious

一 七 切 切 切 切 切

	ON readings リツ RITSU, リュウ RYŪ KUN readings たーつ ta-tsu, たーてる ta-teru	meaning to stand (up)	5 strokes
			radical 立

立

common words

組み立てる	くみたてる	**kumitateru**	to put [fit] together; to assemble
公立の	こうりつの	**kōritsu no**	public; municipal
国立の	こくりつの	**kokuritsu no**	national
逆立ち	さかだち	**sakadachi**	handstand
設立	せつりつ	**setsuritsu**	establishment; foundation
立ち上がる	たちあがる	**tachiagaru**	to get up; to stand up; to rise
独立	どくりつ	**dokuritsu**	independence

＼	亠	亠	立	立	立	立	立

	ON readings キュウ **KYŪ** KUN readings やす－む **yasu-mu,** やす－まる **yasu-maru,** やす－める **yasu-meru**	meaning to rest	6 strokes
			radical 人（イ）

休

common words

休暇	きゅうか	**kyūka**	holiday; day off; vacation
休けい	きゅうけい	**kyūkei**	rest; recess; break; intermission
産休	さんきゅう	**sankyū**	maternity leave
ずる休み	ずるやすみ	**zuruyasumi**	truancy
定休日	ていきゅうび	**teikyūbi**	regular holiday
ひと休み	ひとやすみ	**hito-yasumi**	break; (short) rest
連休	れんきゅう	**renkyū**	consecutive holidays

ノ イ イ 什 什 休 休 休

休

	ON readings ケン **KEN** KUN readings みーる **mi-ru,** みーえる **mi-eru,** みーせる **mi-seru**	meanings to see, to look	7 strokes radical 見

見

common words

見本	みほん	**mihon**	sample; specimen; example; model
意見	いけん	**iken**	opinion; idea; view
見学する	けんがくする	**kengaku suru**	to inspect; to observe
発見	はっけん	**hakken**	discovery
会見	かいけん	**kaiken**	interview
見出し	みだし	**midashi**	headline; heading
見積(もり)	みつもり	**mitsumori**	estimate

丨	冂	月	冃	目	貝	見

見	見					

| | | ON readings
コウ **KŌ**
KUN readings
かんが－える **kanga-eru** | meanings
to think; to con-
sider; to imagine | 6 strokes |
| | | | | radical
老 |

考

common words

選考する	せんこうする	**senkō suru**	to select
考古学	こうこがく	**kōkogaku**	archaeology
参考	さんこう	**sankō**	reference; consultation
思考する	しこうする	**shikō suru**	to think
再考する	さいこうする	**saikō suru**	to reconsider
考え	かんがえ	**kangae**	thinking; idea; thought
考え方	かんがえかた	**kangaekata**	one's way of thinking; one's point of view

一 十 土 耂 考 考 考

考

	ON readings コウ **KŌ**, ギョウ **GYŌ**, アン **AN** **KUN readings** いーく **i-ku**, おこなーう **okona-u**, ゆーく **yu-ku**	**meaning** to go; proceed; conduct	**6 strokes** **radical** 行

行

common words

行く	いく／ゆく	**iku/yuku**	to go; to come
行う	おこなう	**okonau**	to do; to hold; to conduct
売れ行き	うれゆき	**ureyuki**	sales; demand
刊行	かんこう	**kankō**	publication
急行	きゅうこう	**kyūkō**	hurry; express [train]
行事	ぎょうじ	**gyōji**	event; function
銀行	ぎんこう	**ginkō**	bank
犯行	はんこう	**hankō**	crime

ON readings ゲン **GEN,** ゴン **GON** **KUN readings** いーう **i-u,** こと **koto**	**meaning** speech; statement; to say	**7 strokes** **radical** 言

言

common words

合い言葉	あいことば	**aikotoba**	password; watchword; countersign
言い訳	いいわけ	**iiwake**	excuse
言葉	ことば	**kotoba**	language, speech
助言	じょげん	**jogen**	advice
方言	ほうげん	**hōgen**	dialect
寝言	ねごと	**negoto**	nonsense
無言	むごん	**mugon**	silence

		ON readings サク SAKU, サ SA KUN readings つく－る tsuku-ru	meaning a work, to make, create	7 strokes
				radical 人（イ）

作

common words

原作	げんさく	**gensaku**	the original (work)
手作りの	てづくりの	**tezukuri no**	handmade; homemade
作者	さくしゃ	**sakusha**	author; writer
作成する	さくせいする	**sakusei suru**	to make; to prepare; to draw up
作品	さくひん	**sakuhin**	(piece of) work
作文	さくぶん	**sakubun**	composition
作法	さほう	**sahō**	manners; etiquette
名作	めいさく	**meisaku**	masterpiece

ノ イ イ 作 作 作 作

作 作

ON readings チ **CHI** **KUN readings** しーる **shi-ru**	**meanings** to know; news; information; acquaintance; wisdom	**8 strokes**	
		radical 矢	

知

common words

告知	こくち	**kokuchi**	notice
承知	しょうち	**shōchi**	to know; to understand
お知らせ	おしらせ	**oshirase**	word; news; report; notice
知り合い	しりあい	**shiriai**	acquaintance
知恵	ちえ	**chi'e**	wisdom
知能	ちのう	**chinō**	intelligence
通知	つうち	**tsūchi**	notice; notification
未知の	みちの	**michi no**	unknown; strange

ノ	⊢	仁	夕	矢	知	知	知

知	知	知

	ON readings	meanings	9 strokes
	シ **SHI** **KUN readings** おもーう **omo-u**	consideration; thought; to think	**radical** 心

思

common words

思い出す	おもいだす	**omoidasu**	to remember; to recall
思いやり	おもいやり	**omoiyari**	consideration for
不思議な	ふしぎな	**fushigi na**	strange; mysterious
思い切った	おもいきった	**omoikitta**	drastic
思い付き	おもいつき	**omoitsuki**	idea; a plan
思い掛けない	おもいがけない	**omoigakenai**	unexpected; unforeseen
意思	いし	**ishi**	mind; intention

丨	冂	冂	甲	田	田	思	思

思	思	思	思				

ON readings	meaning	9 strokes
ショク SHOKU, ジキ JIKI	food; to eat	radical
KUN readings		食
くーう ku-u, くーらう ku-rau, たーべる ta-beru		

食

common words

外食	がいしょく	**gaishoku**	eat out
給食	きゅうしょく	**kyūshoku**	(school) lunch
軽食	けいしょく	**keishoku**	light meal; snack
食事	しょくじ	**shokuji**	meal
食欲	しょくよく	**shokuyoku**	appetite
食器	しょっき	**shokki**	tableware
食べ物	たべもの	**tabemono**	food
和食	わしょく	**washoku**	Japanese food; Japanese cuisine

ノ 人 仒 今 今 舎 飠 飠

食 食 食 食

	ON readings ライ **RAI** KUN readings くーる **ku-ru,** きーたる **ki-taru,** きーたす **ki-tasu**	meanings to come; since; next	7 strokes radical 木

来

common words

以来	いらい	**irai**	since (then)
再来月	さらいげつ	**saraigetsu**	the month after next
再来年	さらいねん	**sarainen**	the year after next
未来	みらい	**mirai**	future
将来	しょうらい	**shōrai**	future; prospects
出来上がる	できあがる	**dekiagaru**	to be completed
出来る	できる	**dekiru**	can [to be able to]; to be made; to be born

一	一	끼	끄	平	来	来	来
来	来						

	ON readings キ **KI** KUN readings かえ－る **kae-ru,** かえ－す **kae-su**	meanings to return; to come back; to leave	10 strokes
			radical 巾

common words

帰宅する	きたくする	**kitaku suru**	to come home; to go home
帰国する	きこくする	**kikoku suru**	to go [come] back to one's own country; to go [come] (back) home
帰り道	かえりみち	**kaerimichi**	the way home [back]
お帰りなさい	おかえりなさい	**Okaerinasai!**	Welcome home [back]!

ON readings	meanings	10 strokes
ツウ **TSŪ**	authority; ex-	
KUN readings	pert; to go	**radical**
かよ−う **kayo-u,** とお−る **tō-ru,**	along; to pass	辶
とお−す **tō-su**		

通

common words

共通の	きょうつうの	**kyōtsū no**	common; mutual
交通	こうつう	**kōtsū**	traffic; transportation
食通	しょくつう	**shokutsū**	gourmet
通貨	つうか	**tsūka**	currency; money
通信	つうしん	**tsūshin**	communication; correspondence; news
通訳	つうやく	**tsūyaku**	interpretation; interpreter
通路	つうろ	**tsūro**	passage; aisle
普通	ふつう	**futsū**	usually; commonly; ordinary

	ON readings キョウ **KYŌ** KUN readings おし－える **oshi-eru,** おそ－わる **oso-waru**	meaning to teach; to instruct	11 strokes
			radical 攵（攵）

教

common words

教育	きょういく	**kyōiku**	education; training; discipline
教会	きょうかい	**kyōkai**	church
教科書	きょうかしょ	**kyōkasho**	textbook
教師	きょうし	**kyōshi**	teacher; instructor; master
教授	きょうじゅ	**kyōju**	professor
教養	きょうよう	**kyōyō**	culture
仏教	ぶっきょう	**Bukkyō**	Buddhism

			7 strokes
	ON readings バイ **BAI** **KUN readings** うーる **u-ru**, うーれる **u-reru**	**meaning** to sell	
			radical 士

売

common words

売り上げ・売上	うりあげ	**uriage**	sales
売り切れ	うりきれ	**urikire**	sold out; out of stock
売り飛ばす	うりとばす	**uritobasu**	to sell off; to dispose of
小売り	こうり	**ko'uri**	retail
前売り	まえうり	**mae'uri**	advance sale
売店	ばいてん	**baiten**	a stall; a stand; booth
発売する	はつばいする	**hatsubai suru**	to sell; to put on sale
商売	しょうばい	**shōbai**	business; commerce; trade

	ON readings バイ **BAI** KUN readings かーう **ka-u**	meanings to buy; to pur- chase	12 strokes
			radical 貝

買

common words

買価	ばいか	**baika**	purchase price
買い付け	かいつけ	**kaitsuke**	buying; purchasing
買いだめ	かいだめ	**kaidame**	stock up
買い主	かいぬし	**kainushi**	buyer; purchaser
買い物	かいもの	**kaimono**	shopping; purchase
買い占める	かいしめる	**kaishimeru**	to buy up; to corner
買い得	かいどく	**kaidoku**	bargain

	ON readings		meanings	14 strokes
	カ KA		song; poem; verse	radical
	KUN readings			欠
	うた uta, うた−う uta-u			

歌

common words

歌声	うたごえ	**utagoe**	singing voice
歌曲	かきょく	**kakyoku**	song; melody; tune
歌劇	かげき	**kageki**	opera
歌詞	かし	**kashi**	words
国歌	こっか	**kokka**	national anthem
賛美歌	さんびか	**sanbika**	hymn
詩歌	しいか	**shiika**	poetry; poems

一	一	戸	豆	可	可	哥	哥
1	2	3	4	5	6	7	8

哥	哥	哥	歌	歌	歌	歌	歌
9	10	11	12	13	14		

歌

ON readings ショ **SHO** KUN readings かーく **ka-ku**	meanings handwriting; calligraphy; book; letter	10 strokes
		radical 日

書

common words

葉書	はがき	**hagaki**	postcard
書留	かきとめ	**kakitome**	registered mail
肩書	かたがき	**katagaki**	title; degree; position
落書き	らくがき	**rakugaki**	scribbling; graffiti
辞書	じしょ	**jisho**	dictionary
証明書	しょうめいしょ	**shōmeisho**	certificate
秘書	ひしょ	**hisho**	(private) secretary
書類	しょるい	**shorui**	documents

ON readings	meaning	14 strokes
ドク DOKU, トク TOKU, トウ TŌ	to read	radical
KUN readings		言
よーむ yo-mu		

読

common words

読書	どくしょ	**dokusho**	reading
読者	どくしゃ	**dokusha**	reader; subscriber
秒読み	びょうよみ	**byōyomi**	countdown
読み物	よみもの	**yomimono**	reading material; book
朗読	ろうどく	**rōdoku**	reading aloud; recitation
速読	そくどく	**sokudoku**	rapid [speed] reading
愛読書	あいどくしょ	**aidokusho**	one's favorite book

		ON readings ブン **BUN,** モン **MON** KUN readings き－く **ki-ku,** き－こえる **ki-koeru**	meanings to hear; to listen to; to obey; to ask	14 strokes radical 耳

聞

common words

聞き出す	ききだす	**kikidasu**	to get (information) out of; to find out
聞き手	ききて	**kikite**	listener; audience; questioner; interviewer
聞き取り	ききとり	**kikitori**	listening (comprehension)
聞き流す	ききながす	**kikinagasu**	to take no notice of; to ignore
言い聞かせる	いいきかせる	**iikikaseru**	to tell; to persuade, to advise
盗み聞き	ぬすみぎき	**nusumigiki**	eavesdropping
風聞	ふうぶん	**fūbun**	rumor

ON readings	meaning	12 strokes
カイ **KAI**	to open	
KUN readings		radical
あーく **a-ku,** あーける **a-keru,** ひらーく		門
hira-ku, ひらーける **hira-keru**		

開

common words

開催する	かいさいする	**kaisai suru**	to hold; to open
開始する	かいしする	**kaishi suru**	to begin; to start
開発	かいはつ	**kaihatsu**	development; exploitation
公開する	こうかいする	**kōkai suru**	to open (a place) to the public; exhibit (a painting)
再開する	さいかいする	**saikai suru**	to reopen; to resume
再開発	さいかいはつ	**saikaihatsu**	redevelopment
未開の	みかいの	**mikai no**	uncivilized; primitive

1 丨	2 冂	3 冂	4 冃	5 冐	6 門	7 門	8 門
9 門	10 門	11 開	12 開	開	開	開	

	ON readings ヘイ **HEI** KUN readings しーまる **shi-maru,** しーめる **shi-meru,** とーじる **to-jiru,** とーざす **to-zasu**	meanings to shut, to close	11 strokes
			radical 門

閉

common words

開閉	かいへい	**kaihei**	open and shut (a door)
閉まる	しまる	**shimaru**	to be closed; to be shut
閉ざす	とざす	**tozasu**	to shut
閉じ込める	とじこめる	**tojikomeru**	to shut (a person) in [up]
閉じこもる	とじこもる	**tojikomoru**	to shut oneself in
閉鎖する	へいさする	**heisa suru**	to lock out; to close down
閉店	へいてん	**heiten**	close; close down business

	ON readings メイ **MEI,** ミョウ **MYŌ** KUN readings な **na**	meanings name; title; fame; reputation	**6 strokes** radical 口

名

common words

あて名	あてな	**atena**	addressee; address
氏名	しめい	**shimei**	(full) name
しょ名	しょめい	**shomei**	signature; autograph
名前	なまえ	**namae**	name, first name
無名の	むめいの	**mumei no**	nameless; unknown
名画	めいが	**meiga**	masterpiece; excellent film
名刺	めいし	**meishi**	name card; business card
有名な	ゆうめいな	**yūmei na**	famous; well-known

ノ ク タ タ 名 名 名 名

名

			ON readings ト **TO**, ツ **TSU** KUN readings みやこ **miyako**		meanings capital; metropolis	**11 strokes**
						radical 阝

都

common words

首都	しゅと	**shuto**	capital (city); metropolis
都合	つごう	**tsugō**	convenience
都会の	とかいの	**tokai no**	urban; city
都市	とし	**toshi**	city; town
都心	としん	**toshin**	center of a city; the downtown area
都立の	とりつの	**toritsu no**	metropolitan; municipal
不都合な	ふつごうな	**futsugō na**	inconvenient
京都(市)	きょうと(し)	**Kyōto (shi)**	(City of) Kyoto

	ON readings コク **KOKU** KUN readings くに **kuni**	meaning country	8 strokes
			radical □

国

common words

国際的	こくさいてき	**kokusaiteki**	international
国産の	こくさんの	**kokusan no**	domestic; domestically produced
国家	こっか	**kokka**	state; country; nation
外国の	がいこくの	**gaikoku no**	foreign
国宝	こくほう	**kokuhō**	national treasure
国連	こくれん	**Kokuren**	the United Nations
国境	こっきょう	**kokkyō**	border

1 丨	冂 2	3 冃	冃 4	用 5	国 6	国 7	国 8
国	国	国					

	ON readings デン DEN KUN readings		meanings lightning; electricity	13 strokes
				radical 雨

電

common words

乾電池	かんでんち	**kandenchi**	dry cell; battery
静電気	せいでんき	**seidenki**	static electricity
停電	ていでん	**teiden**	power failure [outage]; 　blackout
家電	かでん	**kaden**	home (electronic) appliance
電線	でんせん	**densen**	electric wire
電話	でんわ	**denwa**	telephone; phone
電報	でんぽう	**denpō**	telegram; wire

ON readings ワ **WA** KUN readings はなし **hanashi,** はなーす **hana-su**	meanings story; tale; talk; conversation; topic; rumor	13 strokes radical 言

話

common words

会話	かいわ	**kaiwa**	conversation; talk; dialogue
実話	じつわ	**jitsuwa**	true story
手話	しゅわ	**shuwa**	sign language
神話	しんわ	**shinwa**	myth
世話	せわ	**sewa**	care; help
童話	どうわ	**dōwa**	children's story; fairy tale
話題	わだい	**wadai**	topic; subject

	ON readings ジュウ **JŪ** KUN readings すーむ **su-mu,** すーまう **su-mau**	meaning to live; to reside; dwelling	7 strokes
			radical 人（イ）

住

common words

居住する	きょじゅうする	**kyojū suru**	to live; to reside; to dwell
住居	じゅうきょ	**jūkyo**	house; residence; home
住所	じゅうしょ	**jūsho**	address
住宅	じゅうたく	**jūtaku**	house; residence
住人	じゅうにん	**jūnin**	resident
住民	じゅうみん	**jūmin**	inhabitant; resident
移住	いじゅう	**ijū**	emigration; immigration

ノ　イ　イ　仁　仹　住　住

住　住

		ON readings ショ SHO KUN readings ところ tokoro		meanings place; spot; area; address		8 strokes	

所

common words

教習所	きょうしゅうじょ	**kyōshūjo**	training school
刑務所	けいむしょ	**keimusho**	prison; jail
所在地	しょざいち	**shozaichi**	location; position; site
所得	しょとく	**shotoku**	income; earnings
台所	だいどころ	**daidōkoro**	kitchen
長所	ちょうしょ	**chōsho**	strong [good] point
場所	ばしょ	**basho**	place; spot; scene
役所	やくしょ	**yakusho**	government [public] office

radical

戸

一₁	ラ₂	ヨ₃	戸₄	戸₅	所₆	所₇	所₈
所	所	所					

	ON readings シ **SHI** KUN readings いち **ichi**	meanings city; town; market	5 strokes
			radical 巾

市

common words

市場	いちば	**ichiba**	market (place)
市街	しがい	**shigai**	the streets; city; town
市営の	しえいの	**shiei no**	municipal; city
市民	しみん	**shimin**	resident (of a city); citizen
市役所	しやくしょ	**shiyakusho**	town [city] hall
やみ市	やみいち	**yami'ichi**	black market

	ON readings		meanings		4 strokes
	ク **KU**		ward; section		
	KUN readings				**radical**
					匚

区

common words

区役所	くやくしょ	**kuyakusho**	ward office
区画	くかく	**kukaku**	division; section; block; boundary
区切り	くぎり	**kugiri**	end; stop; pause; period
区長	くちょう	**kuchō**	the head [chief] of a ward
区分	くぶん	**kubun**	division; (a) classification
区別	くべつ	**kubetsu**	difference; distinction
地区	ちく	**chiku**	area; zone

一　丁　又　区　区　区　区

ON readings チョウ CHŌ KUN readings まち machi	meanings town; block; city; street	7 strokes
		radical 田

町

common words

裏町	うらまち	**uramachi**	back-street district
町中	まちなか	**machinaka**	the downtown area; the central area of a town
町内会	ちょうないかい	**chōnaikai**	neighborhood association
町議会	ちょうぎかい	**chōgikai**	town council
町長	ちょうちょう	**chōchō**	town mayor
横町	よこちょう	**yokochō**	alley

	ON readings ブ **BU** KUN readings	meanings part; division; department	11 strokes radical 阝

部

common words

一部	いちぶ	**ichibu**	part; a copy; a volume
外部の	がいぶの	**gaibu no**	outside; external
支部	しぶ	**shibu**	branch office; local (branch)
全部	ぜんぶ	**zenbu**	all; the whole
内部	ないぶ	**naibu**	the interior; the inside (of)
部員	ぶいん	**bu'in**	the staff; member
部長	ぶちょう	**buchō**	[general] manager
部屋	へや	**heya**	room; stable

	ON readings カイ **KAI**, エ **E** KUN readings あーう **a-u**	meanings meeting; party; society; to see; to meet	6 strokes
			radical 人(イ)

会

common words

委員会	いいんかい	**i'inkai**	committee; committee meeting
会員	かいいん	**kai'in**	member of ...; the membership
会議	かいぎ	**kaigi**	meeting; conference
集会	しゅうかい	**shūkai**	meeting; gathering; assembly
会社	かいしゃ	**kaisha**	company; firm; corporation
会場	かいじょう	**kaijō**	hall; meeting place
協会	きょうかい	**kyōkai**	society; association

ノ 人 仐 仐 会 会 会 会

会

	ON readings シャ SHA KUN readings やしろ yashiro	meanings company; firm; corporation; shrine	7 strokes
			radical 示（ネ）

社

common words

社長	しゃちょう	**shachō**	president
支社	ししゃ	**shisha**	branch office
社員	しゃいん	**sha'in**	employee; the staff
社会	しゃかい	**shakai**	society; community
商社	しょうしゃ	**shōsha**	business company [firm]; 　trading company
神社	じんじゃ	**jinja**	(Shinto) shrine
本社	ほんしゃ	**honsha**	the head [main] office

丶₁　　ラ₂　　ネ₃　　ネ₄　　ネ一₅　　衤₆　　社₇

社　社

	ON readings		meanings	6 strokes
	チ CHI, ジ JI		earth; land; ground	
	KUN readings			radical
				土

地

common words

地下鉄	ちかてつ	**chikatetsu**	subway
土地	とち	**tochi**	land; soil
裏地	うらじ	**uraji**	lining
基地	きち	**kichi**	base; military base
原産地	げんさんち	**gensanchi**	place of origin
心地よい	ここちよい	**kokochiyoi**	comfortable; pleasant
下地	したじ	**shitaji**	groundwork; a foundation
大地	だいち	**daichi**	the Earth

一 十 土 圠 坢 地 地 地

地

		ON readings ズ **ZU,** ト **TO** KUN readings はかーる **haka-ru**		meanings picture, draw- ing; figure; illus- tration; chart	7 strokes
					radical □

図

common words

合図	あいず	**aizu**	signal; sign; gesture
指図する	さしずする	**sashizu suru**	to direct; to instruct
図形	ずけい	**zukei**	figure; diagram
図面	ずめん	**zumen**	drawing; plan
地図	ちず	**chizu**	map; atlas
図書館	としょかん	**toshokan**	library
見取り図	みとりず	**mitorizu**	(rough) sketch

	ON readings テン TEN KUN readings みせ mise	meanings store, shop	8 strokes
			radical 广

店

common words

支店	してん	**shiten**	branch (office/store)
商店	しょうてん	**shōten**	shop; store
書店	しょてん	**shoten**	bookstore; bookshop
店員	てんいん	**ten'in**	shop assistant; (store) clerk
店主	てんしゅ	**tenshu**	shopkeeper
百貨店	ひゃっかてん	**hyakkaten**	department store
夜店	よみせ	**yomise**	night stall

丶	亠	广	庁	庄	庄	店	店

| 店 | 店 | 店 | | | | | |

	ON readings		meanings	15 strokes
	オウ Ō		width; breadth; side	
	KUN readings			**radical**
	よこ yoko			木

横

common words

横断歩道	おうだんほどう	**ōdanhodō**	pedestrian crossing; crosswalk
横切る	よこぎる	**yokogiru**	to cross
横たわる	よこたわる	**yokotawaru**	to lie (down)
横取りする	よこどりする	**yokodori suru**	to steal; to snatch (away)
横向きに(の)	よこむきに(の)	**yokomuki ni (no)**	sideways; sidewise
横文字	よこもじ	**yokomoji**	the Roman alphabet; Western language

一	十	才	木	杧	杧	杧	横
杧	槽	楠	構	横	横	横	横
横	横						

ON readings	meanings	9 strokes
シツ SHITSU	room; apartment	radical
KUN readings		宀
むろ muro		

室

common words

温室	おんしつ	**onshitsu**	greenhouse
客室	きゃくしつ	**kyakushitsu**	guest room
教室	きょうしつ	**kyōshitsu**	classroom; schoolroom
個室	こしつ	**koshitsu**	private room; single (room)
寝室	しんしつ	**shinshitsu**	bedroom
地下室	ちかしつ	**chikashitsu**	basement
浴室	よくしつ	**yokushitsu**	bathroom
和室	わしつ	**washitsu**	Japanese-style room

	ON readings カ **KA**, ケ **KE** **KUN readings** いえ **ie**, −や **-ya**, うち **uchi**	**meanings** house; home; family	**10 strokes** **radical** 宀

家

common words

大家	おおや	**ōya**	landlord
画家	がか	**gaka**	painter
家具	かぐ	**kagu**	furniture
家族	かぞく	**kazoku**	family
家庭	かてい	**katei**	home; family; household
作家	さっか	**sakka**	novelist; writer; author
農家	のうか	**nōka**	farmhouse

		ON readings コウ **KŌ**, ク **KU** KUN readings		meanings work; construc- tion; manufac- turing	**3 strokes** radical エ

工

		common words			
		加工食品	かこうしょくひん	**kakōshokuhin**	processed food
		工夫	くふう	**kufū**	device; invention
		工業	こうぎょう	**kōgyō**	industry; manufacturing
		工事	こうじ	**kōji**	construction
		細工	さいく	**saiku**	work; workmanship; 　handiwork
		人工の	じんこうの	**jinkō no**	artificial; man-made
		大工	だいく	**daiku**	carpentry; carpenter

		ON readings ジョウ **JŌ** KUN readings ば **ba**		meanings place; spot		**12 strokes**	
						radical 土	

場

common words

工場	こうじょう	**kōjō**	factory; plant
酒場	さかば	**sakaba**	bar; pub
職場	しょくば	**shokuba**	one's place of work
砂場	すなば	**sunaba**	sandpit; sandbox
戦場	せんじょう	**senjō**	battlefield
入場券	にゅうじょうけん	**nyūjōken**	admission ticket
場合	ばあい	**ba'ai**	case; occasion; circumstances; conditions
穴場	あなば	**anaba**	good unknown spot [place]

一 十 土 圿 圽 圽 圽 坦

坦 場 場 場 場 場 場

	ON readings ドウ **DŌ**, トウ **TŌ** KUN readings みち **michi**		meanings road; street; district; avenue; boulevard; path; way; course	12 strokes
				radical 辶

道

common words

街道	かいどう	**kaidō**	highway
片道	かたみち	**katamichi**	one way
国道	こくどう	**kokudō**	national highway [road, route]
小道	こみち	**komichi**	lane; path; trail; alley
鉄道	てつどう	**tetsudō**	railroad; railway
道具	どうぐ	**dōgu**	tool; instrument; utensil; equipment
道路	どうろ	**dōro**	road; street

				公

ON readings	meanings	4 strokes
コウ **KŌ**	public, official	
KUN readings		**radical**
おおやけ **o'oyake**		八

common words

公園	こうえん	**kō'en**	park
公演	こうえん	**kō'en**	public performance
公害	こうがい	**kōgai**	(environmental) pollution
公会堂	こうかいどう	**kōkaidō**	public hall; civic hall
公共の	こうきょうの	**kōkyō no**	common; public
公式	こうしき	**kōshiki**	formula; formality
公衆電話	こうしゅうでんわ	**kōshū denwa**	public telephone; pay phone

ノ	八	公	公	公	公	公	

ON readings	meanings	4 strokes
ブン **BUN**, モン **MON**	sentence; writing	radical
KUN readings		文
ふみ **fumi**		

文

common words

異文化の	いぶんかの	**ibunka no**	intercultural; cross-cultural
序文	じょぶん	**jōbun**	preface
文句	もんく	**monku**	words; objection; complaint
注文	ちゅうもん	**chūmon**	order
文化	ぶんか	**bunka**	culture
文章	ぶんしょう	**bunshō**	sentence; writing; composition
文法	ぶんぽう	**bunpō**	grammar

文 文 文 文

	ON readings ブツ **BUTSU**, モツ **MOTSU** KUN readings もの **mono**	meanings thing; article; object	8 strokes radical 牛

物

common words

生き物	いきもの	**ikimono**	living thing [being]; life
贈り物	おくりもの	**okurimono**	gift; present
落とし物	おとしもの	**otoshimono**	lost article
果物	くだもの	**kudamono**	fruit
こわれ物	こわれもの	**kowaremono**	fragile; breakable object
植物	しょくぶつ	**shokubutsu**	plant
書物	しょもつ	**shomotsu**	book
荷物	にもつ	**nimotsu**	luggage; baggage

	ON readings ビョウ **BYŌ,** ヘイ **HEI** KUN readings や－む **ya-mu,** やまい **yamai**	meanings illness; disease	10 strokes
			radical 疒

病

common words

おく病な	おくびょうな	**okubyō na**	cowardly; timid
看病	かんびょう	**kanbyō**	nursing
急病	きゅうびょう	**kyūbyō**	sudden illness
仮病	けびょう	**kebyō**	feigned illness
重病	じゅうびょう	**jūbyō**	serious illness
伝染病	でんせんびょう	**densenbyō**	contagious disease
病院	びょういん	**byōin**	hospital; clinic

	ON readings リョウ **RYŌ** KUN readings		meanings charge; fee; rate; fare; toll	10 strokes
				radical 斗

料

common words

原料	げんりょう	**genryō**	raw materials; material(s)
香料	こうりょう	**kōryō**	spice
材料	ざいりょう	**zairyō**	raw materials; material(s); ingredients
資料	しりょう	**shiryō**	materials; data
送料	そうりょう	**sōryō**	postage; shipping [freight] charges
無料の	むりょうの	**muryō no**	free
料金	りょうきん	**ryōkin**	charge

Radical Index

Japanese—English Index

dekiru できる　出来る　can [to be able to]; to be made; to be born *71*

DEN デン　電　lightning; electricity *86*

denpō でんぽう　電報　telegram; wire *86*

densen でんせん　電線　electric wire *86*

densenbyō でんせんびょう　伝染病　contagious disease *108*

denwa でんわ　電話　telephone; phone *86*

deru でる　出る　to come out; to go out; to attend; to participate (in) *55*

DŌ ドウ　動　to move *15*

DŌ ドウ　道　road; street; avenue; way; course *104*

dōbutsu どうぶつ　動物　animal *15*

dōgu どうぐ　道具　tool; instrument; utensil; equipment *104*

DOKU ドク　読　to read *79*

dokuritsu どくりつ　独立　independence *61*

dokusha どくしゃ　読者　reader; subscriber *79*

dokusho どくしょ　読書　reading *79*

dōraku どうらく　道楽　hobby; dissipation *34*

dōro どうろ　道路　road; street *104*

dōshi どうし　動詞　verb *15*

dōwa どうわ　童話　children's story; fairy tale *87*

E

E エ　会　meeting; party; society *94*

ehon えほん　絵本　picture book *18*

EI エイ　英　England; English *26*

eibun えいぶん　英文　English language text *26*

ei'en えいえん　永遠　eternity; permanence *37*

eigo えいご　英語　English *26*

eijishinbun えいじしんぶん　英字新聞　English newspaper *27*

eikaiwa えいかいわ　英会話　English conversation *26*

Eikoku えいこく　英国　England; the United Kingdom *26*

eiwajiten えいわじてん　英和辞典　English-Japanese dictionary *26*

eiyaku えいやく　英訳　translation into English *26*

eiyū えいゆう　英雄　hero *26*

EN エン　遠　far; distant *37*

enchō suru えんちょうする　延長する　to extend *39*

enryo suru えんりょする　遠りょする　refrain; hesitate *37*

ensoku えんそく　遠足　excursion; outing; picnic *37*

F

fuan ふあん　不安　anxiety; worry *50*

fubenkyō na ふべんきょうな　不勉強な　idle; lazy *28*

fūbun ふうぶん　風聞　rumor *80*

fukushū ふくしゅう　復習　review *31*

fumi ふみ　文　sentence; writing *106*

furuboketa ふるぼけた　古ぼけた　grow old *36*

furuhon ふるほん　古本　second-hand [used] book *36*

furui ふるい　古い　old; old-fashioned; stale *36*

furukusai ふるくさい　古くさい　old-fashioned; stale *36*

furusu ふるす　古す　used *36*

fushigi na ふしぎな　不思議な　strange; mysterious *69*

fūshū ふうしゅう　風習　manners; customs *31*

futoi ふとい　太い　fat; thick; deep (voice); bold (lines) *47*

futoji ふとじ　太字　boldface (type) *47*

futomomo ふともも　太もも　thigh *47*

futoru ふとる　太る　to grow fat *47*

futotta ふとった　太った　fat *47*

futsū ふつう　普通　usually; commonly; ordinary *73*

futsugō na ふつごうな　不都合な　inconvenient *84*

G

gaibu no がいぶの　外部の　outside; external *93*

gaikoku no がいこくの　外国の　foreign *85*

gaishoku がいしょく　外食　eat out *70*

gaka がか　画家　painter *101*

gakka がっか　学科　subject; course *23*

gakkō がっこう　学校　school *22*

GAKU ガク　学　learning, studies; science *21*

GAKU ガク　楽　music *34*

gakudan がくだん　楽団　band; orchestra *34*

gakufu がくふ　楽譜　score *34*

gakumon がくもん　学問　studies *32*

gakusei がくせい　学生　student *21*

gakusha がくしゃ　学者　scholar *21*

gakushū がくしゅう　学習　learning; study *31*

gakushū suru がくしゅうする　学習する　to learn; to study *21*

gakuya がくや　楽屋　dressing room *34*

ganka がんか　眼科　ophthalmology *23*

GEN ゲン　言　speech; statement *66*

gengo げんご　言語　language; speech *25*

genryō げんりょう　原料　raw materials; material(s) *109*

gensaku げんさく　原作　original (work) *67*

gensanchi げんさんち　原産地　place of origin *96*

genshō suru げんしょうする　減少する　to decrease *46*

gimon ぎもん　疑問　doubt; question *32*

ginkō ぎんこう　銀行　bank *65*

GO ゴ　語　word; language; speech *25*

GŌ ゴウ　強　strong *29*

gogaku ごがく　語学　language study *25*

gōin na ごういんな　強引な　forcible *56*

gōin ni ごういんに　強引に　by force, forcibly *29*

GON ゴン　言　speech; statement *66*

goraku ごらく　娯楽　amusement; recreation *34*

GYO ギョ　魚　fish *12*

GYŌ ギョウ　行　to go *65*

gyōji ぎょうじ　行事　event; function *65*

gyokai ぎょかい　魚介　seafood *12*

GYŪ ギュウ　牛　cow; bull *11*

gyūdon ぎゅうどん　牛丼　a bowl of rice topped with cooked beef *11*

gyūgawa ぎゅうがわ　牛革　cowskin; calfskin *11*

gyūniku ぎゅうにく　牛肉　beef *11*

gyūnyū ぎゅうにゅう　牛乳　milk *11*

H

habahiroi はばひろい　幅広い　wide; broad *49*

haeru はえる　生える　to come up; to grow *19*

hagaki はがき　葉書　postcard *78*

hairu はいる　入る　to enter *54*

hakaru はかる　図る　to plan; to measure; to attempt; to try; to devise *97*

hakken はっけん　発見　discovery *63*

hanashi はなし　話　story; tale; talk *87*

hanasu はなす　話す　to talk; to speak *87*

hankō はんこう　犯行　crime *65*

hashiru はしる　走る　to run *58*

hatsubai suru はつばいする　発売する　to sell; to put on sale *75*

hatsumei はつめい　発明　invention *53*

hayai はやい　速い　quick; fast; rapid; speedy; prompt *41*

hayai はやい　早い　early; soon; fast; rapid; quick *52*

hayamaru はやまる　早まる　be hasty; be advanced *52*

hayameru はやめる　速める　to quicken *41*

hayameru はやめる　早める　to speed up; to hasten *41*

kokkyō こっきょう 国境 border *85*

kōkō こうこう 高校 high school *22*

kokochiyoi ここちよい 心地よい comfortable; pleasant *96*

kōkogaku こうこがく 考古学 archaeology *64*

kōkoku こうこく 広告 advertisement; notice *49*

KOKU コク 国 country *85*

kokuchi こくち 告知 notice *68*

kokudō こくどう 国道 national highway [road, route] *104*

kokugo こくご 国語 Japanese language; national language *25*

kokuhō こくほう 国宝 national treasure *85*

Kokuren こくれん 国連 the United Nations *85*

kokuritsu no こくりつの 国立の national *61*

kokusaiteki こくさいてき 国際的 international *85*

kokusan no こくさんの 国産の domestic; domestically produced *85*

kōkyō no こうきょうの 公共の common; public *105*

kōkyū na こうきゅうな 高級な high-quality; luxury *51*

komainu こまいぬ こま犬 a pair of stone guardian dogs (at the gate of a Shinto shrine) *10*

komichi こみち 小道 lane; path; trail; alley *104*

komoji こもじ 小文字 small letter *27*

komugi こむぎ 小麦 wheat *44*

konomi このみ 好み liking; taste; choice; preference *30*

konomu このむ 好む like, be fond of; prefer *30*

kō'on こうおん 高温 high temperature *51*

kōritsu no こうりつの 公立の public; municipal *61*

kōryō こうりょう 香料 spice *109*

kōsei こうせい 校正 proofreading *22*

kōsha こうしゃ 校舎 school building *22*

kōshiki こうしき 公式 formula; formality *105*

koshitsu こしつ 個室 private room; single (room) *100*

kōshū denwa こうしゅうでんわ 公衆電話 public telephone; pay phone *105*

kōsoku こうそく 高速 high [full] speed *41*

kotae こたえ 答 answer *33*

kotaeru こたえる 答える to answer *33*

kōtei こうてい 校庭 school grounds *22*

koten こてん 古典 classic *36*

koto こと 言 word; speech; expression *66*

kotoba ことば 言葉 language, speech *66*

kotori ことり 小鳥 small bird *13*

kōtsū こうつう 交通 traffic; transportation *73*

kōtsugō na こうつごうな 好都合な convenient *30*

ko'uri こうり 小売り retail *75*

kowaremono こわれもの こわれ物 fragile; breakable object *107*

koyubi こゆび 小指 pinkie (finger) *44*

kōzan こうざん 高山 high mountain *51*

kozukai こづかい 小づかい pocket money *44*

kozutsumi こづつみ 小包 package *44*

KU ク 区 ward; section *91*

KU ク 工 work; construction; manufacturing *102*

kubetsu くべつ 区別 difference; distinction *91*

kubun くぶん 区分 division; (a) classification *91*

kuchibashiru くちばしる 口走る to blurt out; to babble *58*

kuchō くちょう 区長 head [chief] of a ward *91*

kudamono くだもの 果物 fruit *107*

kufū くふう 工夫 device; invention *102*

kugiri くぎり 区切り end; stop; pause; period *91*

kukaku くかく 区画 division; section; block; boundary *91*

kumitateru くみたてる 組み立てる to put [fit] together; to assemble *61*

kuni くに 国 country *85*

kurau くらう 食らう to eat, to drink *70*

kuru くる 来る to come *71*

ku'u くう 食う to eat, to consume *70*

kuyakusho くやくしょ 区役所 ward office *91*

kyakushitsu きゃくしつ 客室 guest room *100*

KYŌ キョウ 強 strong *29*

KYŌ キョウ 教 to teach; to instruct *74*

kyōiku きょういく 教育 education; training; discipline *74*

kyōju きょうじゅ 教授 professor *74*

kyojū suru きょじゅうする 居住する to live; to reside; to dwell *88*

kyōka きょうか 教科 subject; course of study; curriculum *23*

kyōkai きょうかい 教会 church *74*

kyōkai きょうかい 協会 society; association *94*

kyōkasho きょうかしょ 教科書 textbook *74*

kyōka suru きょうかする 強化する to strengthen *29*

kyōshi きょうし 教師 teacher; instructor; master *74*

kyōshitsu きょうしつ 教室 classroom; schoolroom *100*

kyōshūjo きょうしゅうじょ 教習所 training school *89*

kyōsō きょうそう 競走 race *58*

Kyōto(shi) きょうと(し) 京都 (市) (city of) Kyoto *84*

kyōtsū no きょうつうの 共通の common; mutual *73*

kyōun きょううん 強運 good luck *29*

kyōyō きょうよう 教養 culture *74*

KYŪ キュウ 休 to rest *62*

kyūbyō きゅうびょう 急病 sudden illness *108*

kyūka きゅうか 休暇 holiday; day off; vacation *62*

kyūkei きゅうけい 休けい rest; recess; break; intermission *62*

kyūkō きゅうこう 急行 hurry; express (train) *65*

kyūshoku きゅうしょく 給食 (school) lunch *70*

kyūsoku na きゅうそくな 急速な rapid *41*

M

machi まち 町 town; city *92*

machidōshii まちどおしい 待ち遠しい be looking forward to *37*

machinaka まちなか 町中 downtown area; central area of a town *92*

mae'uri まえうり 前売り advance sale *75*

makeinu まけいぬ 負け犬 loser *10*

manabu まなぶ 学ぶ to learn *21*

maruta まるた 丸太 log *47*

masani まさに 正に exactly; surely; truly *48*

MEI メイ 明 bright *53*

MEI メイ 名 name; title; fame; reputation *83*

meiga めいが 名画 masterpiece; excellent film *83*

meisaku めいさく 名作 masterpiece *67*

meishi めいし 名刺 name card; business card *83*

michi みち 道 road; street; way *104*

michi no みちの 未知の unknown; strange *68*

midashi みだし 見出し headline; heading *63*

mieru みえる 見える to be able to see *63*

mihon みほん 見本 sample; specimen; example; model *63*

mijikai みじかい 短い short; brief *40*

mijika ni みちかに 身近に close (to) *38*

mikai no みかいの 未開の uncivilized; primitive *81*

minarau みならう 見習う to emulate *31*

mirai みらい 未来 future *71*

miru みる 見る to see, to look, to watch *63*

English–Japanese Index